For every David
facing a Goliath

I hope this book lights a new fire
or fans an old flame.

I hope this book reminds
you of what's possible.

I hope this book brings you face to face with the unknown,
and inspires you to take a step beyond what you thought
was certain.

I hope this book feels like a wind at your back whispering,

"The world needs what you have to offer.
Keep going, keep going, keep going."

I hope this book is a reminder that you
are going somewhere, not just doing
something.

There is more beauty in you than
destruction in the world.

I hope you never stop.

Please, never stop.

dreams
like distant sounds
of battle

call
to me in the
echoes and

beg
me to pick up
my sword

again.

I made a movie with a man who had it all.

The Academy Awards
the money
the influence.

If you saw him, you would know him.

And you probably love his movies.

But, on the plane, no one would sit next to him.

No one liked him.

No one wanted to be next to him.

So, he always sat alone.

I wonder, was it worth the trade?

To have it all

...But sit alone.

If you want a job, there are
things you can do.

But, if you want
a career, there is

someone
you
should
be.

They say...

Nothing arrives until you're prepared.

But what are you preparing the skill, or the person?

It's not about skills.

It's about you.

That's what
this book
is about.

They also say...

A career in service to a career
is not a career,
it's a trap.

Do you feel trapped?

You're not supposed to feel that way.

That's what
this book
is about.

This book offers an organic approach to
career that will change
the way you relate

to the hustle,

to the industry,

and to the actor

you want to become.

It will take the power from the
people who manage it, and
put it back in
the hands of the actors
who create it.

This is what you've
been looking for.

Here's the good news:

Yes.

You can have the career you want
without losing the person you are.

It's possible.

It's totally possible.

This book will
show you
how.

There are two ways to see your acting career.

Two ways to order your house.

Two ways to guide your decisions.

Two ways.

1. CORPORATE ECONOMY
2. CREATIVE ECONOMY

"ECONOMY" is come from the Greek: Oikos + Nomos

Oikonomia

It means: the ruling order of your house.

The way you live your life. The ruling principles that guide your decision- making and risk-taking.

The way you see the world.

Your personal economy.

Corporate Economy

If/then.

Yeah, but.

Either, or.

Right, wrong.

Never enough.

If the Corporate Economy
was on a dating app,

Here are the 5 things it
would tell you about itself.

(Would you swipe right or left?)

1. It's Transactional.

You know, like buying a stamp. I give you a nickel, and you give me a stamp.

I do THIS, and you give me THAT.

It works sometimes.

Like when you're buying a stamp.

But not when you're
making a career
in acting.

2. It Divides.

Take a blueberry muffin.

Chop it into pieces.

Small pieces.

Throw it to the birds.

Then watch them fight over it.

That's what your career
looks like in a
corporate economy.

3. It Encourages Deceit.

I'll tell you anything
To get what I want.

But you won't believe what I tell you.

Because you'll say anything also.

And you know it.

...Or even worse.

You do believe me.

Because deep down you aren't
sure what you believe

So, you'll trust anyone.

4. It Creates Limited Resources.

There is not enough for everyone.

Do what you can to get what you want.

Every day there is less.

Every day you are less.

Eventually, you will be

Too "old"

Too "fat"

Too "ugly"

And you won't get
anything anymore.

5. It Emphasizes the Power of Results.

It convinces you that you can have an effect before a cause.

Like an ouch without a pinch, juice without the squeeze, and a home run without a swing.

Here's how it works:

People love home runs.

And everyone loves the person who hits them.

Swinging is lame.

People who swing are lame.

Home runs are cool.

People who hit them matter.

(See what I mean?)

Sounds like a great date, right?

Familiar?

Hope not.

But wait.

There's more.

Try this:

Close your eyes, and think about your career.

What comes to mind when you do this?

Do you have images of your success?
Are you excited for the future?

When you close your eyes and think of your career, are you encouraged, are you thrilled, are you satisfied with where your career currently is and is heading?

Or, are you like most actors who have a hard time celebrating their career, and are constantly combating voices of discouragement and limitations?

Or, maybe, when you think of your career, you are a little of both.

Some days are good, some days are bad.

But nothing is consistent.

There can be many discouraging
voices speaking to you
when you think
about your
career.

Some voices are from your past.

Some voices are from your mind.

Some voices are from your friends.

Some voices were given to you.

Some voices were created by you.

But, no matter what, all discouraging voices come from the
Corporate Economy.

When you have a Corporate Economy mindset,

these voices get mixed up, they're all connected,
and it's loud

Here are the 4
loudest Corporate Voices

Doubt

Greed

Fear

Anger

Doubt

The voice of Doubt can take many forms,
but in an actor's career, the voice of doubt
always compares you to others.

Comparison is Doubt

rationalized

vocalized

and believed.

Notice that when you
compare yourself to someone else,
you never come out ahead.

Doubt never says,

"My career is in a great place. I am thrilled to be amongst
these amazing actors. I'm truly one of the lucky ones."

Doubt says,

"My career isn't as good as my friend's career. She has a
better agent, more auditions, and she's younger than me. My
agent sucks, I'm not booking, and I'm past my prime."

The voice of Doubt will only
remind you of what
you are not.

It never brags about
what you are.

Doubt is not the opposite
of confidence;
it is the opposite
of worthiness.

Doubt is like a drill that begins on the surface, but quickly makes its way into the center of your heart.

It begins by drilling into your abilities:

"I'm not sure I have what it takes to book this audition."

Then it quickly begins to drill into who you are:

"I'm not sure I'm good enough to book this audition."

Then, it uses comparison to drill into your self-worth:

"They'll probably cast someone more famous than me."

Pretty soon, what began as a doubt about your ability, has turned into a doubt about your worthiness.

This is how Doubt wins.

The voice of Doubt tells you
that failure is an identity,
not just an event.

The voice of Doubt works
hard to make you less.

(stop
believing
voices
that
make
you
less.)

Greed

Not everything belongs to you.

Not
every job
every opportunity
every agent
every role
every audition
belongs to you.

Any time you want something that does not belong to you

you are listening to the voice of greed.

Greed is not a measure of what you have;
it's a measure of how badly you want
what others have.

Greed
and
jealousy
are
BFFs

Rich people
can be greedy

Poor people
can be greedy

It just depends
on what you want

And whether or not
it belongs to you.

Be careful...

Greed

looks like
desperation

and

smells like
bitterness

but

feels like
reward

and

sounds like
a good
idea

Greed and
generosity
cannot
live in the
same room.

Greed is never fulfilled.

Greed is never finished.

Greed never gets enough.

What you have is not enough because

Who you are is not enough.

Greed tells you that
you are not enough

and that you
can compensate
for your lack
by having
what does not
belong to you.

People who are greedy with money

are also greedy with

Forgiveness

Love

Encouragement

and

all the things that really matter.

Beware.

Are you fighting a fight that
doesn't belong to you?

Are you feeling stress that
doesn't belong to you?

Are you carrying burdens
that don't belong to you?

If so, that's Greed.

Stop fighting that fight. It's not your struggle.

Breathe. It's not your stress to feel.

Put your burdens down. They aren't yours to carry.

They do not belong to you.

You will never find
your strength by carrying the
weight of others.

You
Cannot
Be
Greedy
And
Grateful
At
The
Same
Time

Fear

(i'm scared to write this, btw.)

why?

(because, I'm not sure it will be good.)

so?

(if it's not good you won't like it.)

oh.

(and all my work is an extension of me.)

wait...

(if you don't like my work, it means you don't like me.)

ah.

(so, I'm scared to write this.)

...that's what a fear loop looks like.

Fear happens
when you project a
negative outcome into the future.

If you think tomorrow is gonna suck,
you'll be scared of tomorrow.

If you think your work will be bad,
you'll be scared to create it.

If you think you'll fail,
you'll be too scared to try.

Fear defines your limits.

If you're scared of heights,
you'll stay low.

If you're scared of speaking,
you'll stay quiet.

If you're scared of the future,
you'll stay in the past.

If you're scared of success,
you won't succeed.

Have you heard this voice?

"I haven't booked a role
in a long time...
I probably won't book
this one either..."

That's the
voice of fear.

Past
=
Future

(this is a lie Fear shouts at you)

Careful.

Fear is most
dangerous
when it looks like
wisdom.

Anger

Hold on.

Wait.

There's nothing wrong with being angry.

Anger as a response
as a feeling
as a moment

is ok.

Totally ok.

Anger as a reaction
a lens
a perspective
a default

is not ok.

How do we tell the difference?

Like this:

Anger as a REACTION to something you hate like traffic

(Or your day job
Or your day job
Or your day job)

is useless.

This will lead to
Screaming...Yelling...Tantrums

This anger feels powerful
But only tears people down.

This anger feels good today
but hurts tomorrow.
This anger feels strong,
but leaves you weaker
in
the
long
run.

Anger as a RESPONSE to something you love

Like healing the environment

or feeding starving people

or ending homelessness

or stopping drug abuse

is fruitful.

It might look like

Writing
Thinking
Planning

and will always lead to

Action
Solution
Purpose.

There are lots of "actor" things to be angry at:

The industry
Directors
Casting directors
Producers
Agents
Managers
Writers
Critics

Sometimes anger at these things comes out as complaining about these things.

Complaining is civilized anger.

Complaining is a cancer.

Complaining proves to others that you are not in control.

Stop complaining.

Seriously.

Stop it.

Those are the voices of the Corporate Economy.

You may hear them.

You may ALWAYS hear them.

That's ok.

It's ok to hear them.

Just don't believe them.

The loudest voices are not always the truth.

Like all voices,
the Corporate Economy
voices come
from somewhere.

They are built on something.
They come
from somewhere.

They are resting on a foundation.

Here is the foundation for the Corporate Economy:

Obligation

Individualism

Tasks

Entitlement

Obligation

Obligation
is
a
gratitude
desert.

When
I
"have"
to,

I
forget
what
it's
like
to

"get"

to.

When people live under an oppressive
government regime, they have no choice in their lives.
They must do what they are told...or else.

So, they become very good at **saying** "yes".

But, since they didn't choose to say "yes", they become
very good at **doing** "no".

When you decide to be an actor,
but never behave like one,

when you say "yes", but you do "no", you are being passive
aggressive towards your career. You are behaving out of
obligation.

Your career has become your dictator.

It is telling you what to do.

(it should be the other
way around, you know.)

Obligation leads
to mindless repetition.

Mindless Repetition = Habits

Habits never reveal
our best selves.

If Obligation were a new pill, the commercial would sound like this:

"Are you tired of your meaningful life? Is inspiration making you sick? Are you tired of being so creative?

If so, try the new OBLIGATION NATION PILL!

Guaranteed to make you: feel guilty about your career, build resentment towards your friends, accelerate burnout, throw you into glass ceilings, only do what others tell you, remind you of your insignificance, embarrass you in front of your high school crush at your 10-year reunion, and want to quit it all and get a job in a cubicle so you can fill out forms for the rest of your life!

Consult a casting director, agent, manager, producer, or social media post to get your pill today!"

Fo' real y'all.

Individualism

Individualism loves
these mantras:

I
Can
Do
It
Alone.

I
Am
All
There
Is.

I
Am
The
Only
One
Who
Matters.

Individualism is the prioritization of
MY NEEDS for the sake of
MY NEEDS.

Individualism craves

Instant gratification
Absolute recognition
Pointless notification
Endless glorification

It tells you,

The only relationship that matters,
is the one you have with yourself.

All others become a hobby.

Individualism will
convince you that

Alone > Together

Pride > Humility

Division > Unity

Individualism views
the world according
to these principles:

"I have what you do not."

therefore...

"I am what you are not."

and...

"the more you are not, the more I am."

therefore...

"I am happy and you are not."

"I am loved and you are not."

"I am successful and you are not."

Ever had that friend who "changed" when they got successful?

Yeah.

Like all of a sudden, they were "above" you.

Yeah.

Like they were sitting on a cloud admiring the distanc between you and them.

Yeah.

That's an "individual".

H. Weinstein

(need I say more...?)

Tasks

Tasks are

strategies
goals
steps
lists
activities
should do's
meant to do's
and
need to do's

that have been drained of

art
intention
and
purpose.

Tasks
happen without a why.

They happen
just because.

Tasks are never questioned
evaluated
or reinvented.

You do them

cause
you were told to

or cause
you always did

or cause
others did

or cause
it worked last time.

Tasks are things
you should have said "no" to.

But you didn't.

And now you're stuck.

(hint: It's ok to say "no")

Tasks make you
feel busy,
but are rarely
productive.

Busy

≠

Productive

How to Know You're Too Busy

Do you turn down a lot of invitations?

"Hey! Wanna go watch a play?"

"Can't. I'm busy. Again."

Like you don't have enough time to enjoy life.

Have you bragged about being busy?

"how've you been lately?"

"So busy. Man, I'm so busy. It's great."

Like it's the goal of life or something.

Do people predict your busyness?

"I know you're busy. Just wanted to ask."

Like busy has become your reputation.

If so, you need to check yourself.

Entitlement

When Greed marries Impatience,
they have a baby named Entitlement.

He believes he is owed everything. Even when he didn't earn it.

He wants it now, he wants it all.

It is owed to him.

He never grows up, lives in his own world, and never thinks of anyone else.

He sues people for things that aren't their fault like slamming his finger into a door, or tripping on the stairs.

He believes he deserves according to his presence, not according to his persistence.

When he doesn't get what he wants, he gets bitter, angry, and blames everyone else. It is never his fault.

Entitlement is a brat,
and no one likes him.

You may work
hard for years.

You may do all
the "right things".

You may be the
most talented.

You may know all
the right people.

You may have
what it takes.

You may earn
the right to win.

But, you are never
entitled to it.

Entitlement is the
fast track
to high-grade
bitterness.

There is never a reason to be bitter.

(but, you don't know how hard I worked)

There is never a reason to be bitter.

(but, you don't know what it's like)

There is never a reason to be bitter.

(but, you don't know how long I've been trying)

There is never a reason to be bitter.

(that's easy for you to say)

You're right. It is easy to say. But, it's true.

And, sometimes, the truth is hard to say...but not this time.
This time it's easy to say.

So, I'll say it again.

There is never a reason to be bitter.

Like Obligation, Entitlement is also a gratitude desert.

And

...a humility desert
...a willingness desert
...a collaboration desert
...a creativity desert
...a creation desert.

Nothing good lives
when entitlement is present.

No
One
Owes
You
Any-
thing.

That is the foundation of the Corporate
Economy.

But, don't worry,

The Corporate Economy is not always bad.

It's a great way to organize.

Stop at red lights.
Pay for your coffee.
Follow most rules.

But it's a horrible way to create a career

or art

or a life.

So.

Try this instead.

Creative Economy

If/if.

Yeah, and

Both, and

Right, right

Always enough

If the Creative Economy
was on a dating app...

Here are the 5 things it
would tell you about itself...

(Would you swipe right or left?)

I. It's Transformative.

You know, like when you're on a hike, and you're tired, and it's hot, and you're thirsty, and you're wondering,

why the hell did I go on this hike?

Then you get to the top of the mountain, and you see the view.
You take it all in, you change, you shift

something transforms
things are different

but you can't quite articulate it
all you know
is that all of a sudden

you remember why
you went on the hike.

It's a definitive moment
absent a definitive
definition.

2. It Multiplies.

In the Creative Economy, there is no division.

One idea leads to the
next to the next to the next.

One opportunity leads
to the next to the
next to the next.

All things grow.

There is always enough.

Always one more
seat at the table.

Everything leads to something
and nothing takes
away from anything.

3. It Inspires Generosity

Because there is plenty
Because there is always enough

The Creative Economy inspires a spirit of generosity with all things.

Generosity with the easy things like

Money
Clothes
Food
Coffee

&

Generosity with the hard things like

Attention
Time
Love
Praise

4. It Creates Abundant Resources

There is no such thing as "limited resources".

There is only limitless resourcefulness which creates abundance.

There is always a way

There is always plenty

Your gain is my gain

There is no need to fear;
in the Creative Economy
you never run out.

5. It Nurtures Gratitude

This is the most important character trait of the Creative Economy.

If all the other qualities were thrown into a crock pot and cooked for 10 hours, you would be left with a gumbo of gratitude.

Gratitude is the cashmere blanket that wraps around the Creative Economy.

Gratitude transforms arrogance into self-confidence, anger into forgiveness, and greed into generosity.

Gratitude is the seed of generosity, the root of transformation, the fruit of abundance, and the product of growth.

Gratitude is the context for wonder, the catalyst for discovery, and the essence of presence.

There are voices you hear
when you adopt a Creative Economy Mindset

But, the voices don't yell

They whisper.

So, you have to

listen carefully.

Here are the 4
whispering Creative Voices

Patience

Hope

Generosity

Discipline

Patience

I'm gonna be honest.
It's hard to write about patience.

I've been sitting here for a while.

patient.

I've had a lot of thoughts come to my mind. I've had lots of
analogies.

Lots of metaphors and similes

that I think could illustrate my point.

But, I keep sitting here.

being patient.

Holding out for the right metaphor, analogy, simile.

That's what patience does:
it holds out for what is right, it never holds on to what was
wrong.

...here's hoping it was worth it.

The Hurried Farmer and The Man with The Scar

One day, there was a young farmer who planted an orange seed. For weeks, he waited but the seed never grew.

As he waited he grew frustrated.

So, the young farmer stood above the seed and yelled down into the earth, "Hurry up!! Grow! Grow!! Grow! I want an orange."

An old farmer with a scar across his face heard the young man shouting and came to see what was going on.

As he approached, the young farmer said to the old man, "I planted a seed, and nothing is happening. I've waited for weeks, but now I'm frustrated, so I'm yelling at it, but it still won't grow. Tell me what to do."

The old farmer with the scar looked at the young man and smiled and said, "Stop yelling. You can't rush a seed. Be patient. Water it, till the soil, give it sunlight. Be patient."

The old man's scar made his face look cavernous, dangerous, and a little frightening. But, the young man was too frustrated to notice.

So, he responded, "But, I want the fruit now. I need it now. I'm tired of waiting."

"If you do not have the patience to grow the seed, then you are undeserving of its fruit."

At this, the young man grew quiet. The old man continued.

"The seed grows in the dark and never asks, how much further until I reach the light', it just grows. The seed grows through rocks and roots, and never complains, it's too hard'. The seed never worries whether you will like its fruit, or think its flower is beautiful, the seed just grows. It gives you the fruit of its effort, and you must offer the same. You must choose the right soil, collect the right water, and find the right light. You must tend to it every day, wake up early, and work hard to protect it. A seed will never give to you what you are unwilling to give to it. If you want what is inside the seed, you must give it what is inside of you. And you must never rush it. You must always be patient."

The young man protested, "But I have been patient. I've been waiting for weeks. I wait and wait, and nothing happens."

"Young man, waiting is not the same as being patient. Patience is active caring. Waiting is passive worry. Patience looks forward to the future; waiting only remembers the past. Patience gives time; waiting takes it away. Patience requires the discipline to care. Patience without discipline leads to waiting. You have been waiting, but you are not patient. If you want to wait, set a trap. If you have patience, plant a seed."

The young man opened his eyes wide as a new idea hit him. Then, with a powerful voice, he said, "I will! I will set traps, and I will catch anything that walks into them. And I will catch it quickly."

Then, like water washing through clay, a sideways smile grew across the old man's mouth, stretching the scar on his face.

He looked at the boy and said, "I, too, have set traps. I hid them in the dark where no one could see them, and I waited and waited. Then suddenly, I heard the trap SNAP! I ran to the woods, uncovered my trap, and found waiting for me, a rat. Dead, and bleeding. I cannot eat a rat, so I threw him back and set the trap again. When I heard the next SNAP, I ran to the woods and discovered I'd caught an eagle. But, eagles should not be trapped, so I set him free. The third time I heard the trap, I ran to the woods to find I had trapped a bear. But, I was not ready to catch a bear, so he escaped and gave me this scar."

The young man began to breathe quickly as he finally noticed the scar.

"When you set traps, you never know what you will catch. Many things, like rats, are not worth catching. Other things, like eagles, should not be caught. But, most dangerous of all, you may catch things like bears, that you are not ready to catch. Do not set traps, young man. Plant seeds."

The old man's scar created a shadow over his face as he turned and walked away, leaving the young man alone with his seed.

Patience is the perspective
of all creative
careers.

It is the core
of forgiveness

which is the
essence of
freedom

which unleashes
possibilities.

Possibility is the seed
of dreams

which are the
foundation
of careers

Which takes patience
to realize.

Hope

I was always told about the "fear of failure."

I was always told that fearing failure was a bad thing.

I should get rid of that fear.

But I was never told how.

And a WHAT without a HOW is useless.

So, try this.

Replace fear of failure,
with HOPE for success.

But what is hope?

Hope is a verb before it is a noun.

It's something you must do before it's something you will have.

Hope is many things to many people.

It's the source of goodness, of optimism, and joy.

Hope can keep you alive.

Hope is a survival technique.

Hope projects a positive result into the future.

Hope says tomorrow will be
better than today.

Hope is irrational.

Hope makes no sense.

Hope cannot be proven.

So, careful...

Reasonable people will tell you it's not real.

Reasonable people will tell you to prepare for the worst.

Reasonable people
will tell you to stop dreaming, stop believing, and get real.

It happens all the time.

Reasonable people are good
at finding reasons NOT to do things.

Careful who you listen to.

It's not always good to be reasonable.

Hope
looks
like
dreaming.

There is such a thing as a Hope Loop.

It goes like this.

Hope replaces fear, which opens the door to success, which creates more hope, which creates more success, which creates more hope, which creates more success, which creates more hope, which creates more success, which creates more hope, which creates more success, which creates more hope, which creates more success, which creates more hope, which creates more success, which creates more hope, which creates more success, which creates more hope, which creates more success, which creates more hope, which creates more success, which creates more hope, which creates more success, which creates more hope, which creates more success, which creates more hope.

And that's how you conquer fear of failure.

Generosity

Generosity is
gratitude in
action.

No one can steal what you are
willing to give.

So, you don't need to lock away your

Ideas
Talents
Connections
First drafts
Happiness
Attention
Love

You can set them all free.

You cannot steal
from a generous heart.

Generosity has no catch.

No agenda.

No if/then.

Generosity does not claim ownership, or inspire guilt in the one who receives it.

Generosity is not transactional.

Generosity never asks for anything in return.

Generosity is the only non-possessive form of love.

Isn't that awesome?

Never be scared to give.
Stop protecting what you've made.

Creativity is not a product,
it's a resource.

You can always make more
You can always make more
You can always make more

Generosity is the natural result of
a deeply held
belief that
you
can
always
create
more.

Who Owns Who?

The things we own begin to own
us when we can't give them away.

That goes for cars,
clothes, shoes, food, money

and

That goes for ideas,
art, impulses, attention, time,
and love.

You
are
never
too
poor
to
give.

Discipline

This word feels like an ex-boy/girlfriend.

You know, that boy/girlfriend you always loved, but weren't ready for. The one your friends got along with, the one your mom hoped you'd marry, the one who challenged you in all the right ways.

But you were a kid. Immature, distracted, and aloof. You were impatient, unfaithful, and self-absorbed.

Except you didn't know it, so you blamed them for everything.

Everything was their fault. They were too difficult, they were controlling, manipulating, and bossy. They were hard to get along with, tried to change you, and weren't any fun. They trapped you, and took away your freedom.

So, you broke up with them. Ended things. And you haven't turned back.

Until...
One day you're at a coffee shop, and this ex is sitting at the table across from you.

They're staring at you, inviting you to come sit down. To try again. To give it one more try.

You don't get up. You just sit there and look at them.

Still they invite you to come over and try again.

○ ————— ○ ————— ○

Yeah. It's kind of like that. Discipline is something you know exists, something that is right in front of you, but for some reason, you have a hard time approaching.

Maybe because, a long time ago, you didn't get along with Discipline. Maybe you thought it burned you, or maybe you thought you let it down, or maybe you thought it controlled you.
So, you broke up with it, and swore you'd never go back.

But, now, it's sitting across from you, and you can't ignore it anymore.

It's time to grow up and give it another chance.

Get up and go over there.

Discipline is a pattern for
improvement, not a structure
for enslavement.

Discipline is like a stone
path laid across a
raging river.

Discipline is a boundary
between you and the
chaos around you.

Everything happens
for a reason.

Discipline lets us
affect the reason
they happen.

And, eventually,
your discipline
will be mistaken
for your talent.

Eventually,
your discipline
will be mistaken
for your
genius.

There are 3 different types of Discipline.

1. **Personal.** You know, things like hygiene, alarm clocks, finances, nutrition, and calling your parents on Sunday afternoon.

2. **Professional.** "On time is late", do what you say you'll do when you say you'll do it, be ethical, lock the door behind you.

3. **Communal.** Friends don't let friends slack off. Hold those closest to you accountable.

They're all related.

When one is absent,
the others start to fade.

Thoughts on Personal Discipline

Consider your relationship to these 5 areas of your life

Family
Faith
Finances
Fitness
Friendships

If you were to rank them from 1-10, with 10 indicating the healthiest relationship, how would you rank them?

Then, what patterns, routines, or practices could you implement into your day that will elevate the low numbers, and maintain the high ones?

Call your mom? Meditate differently?
Save money? Eat better?
Schedule a friend date?

This is personal discipline.
It's how you get good at life.

Thoughts on Professional Discipline

Professional discipline is rooted in one thing:

INTEGRITY

In the professional world, integrity is calculated like this:

Do you do what you say you'll do when you say you'll do it?

If so, you have the professional discipline to be of high integrity.

If not, you suck.
(and you may be a bad friend, too.)

Here's a quick way to stay in your integrity:

When you know you can, say "yes".
When you know you can't, say "no".
When you're unsure, ask for clarity.

Integrity is the alignment of your beliefs and your behavior.

Does how you act reflect what you believe? Is what you do a reflection of who you are? Is what you show a reflection of who you are?

Here's a good way to explain it:

Nature is always in its integrity.

When you peel the outside of a banana, you always get a banana on the inside. Imagine if you peeled the outside of a banana, and you got an apple on the inside.

Weird.

Some people are like that. They are not in their integrity. What we see is not always what we get.

They are lacking integrity.

<u>Saying "No".</u>

You cannot do everything.

There is integrity in saying "no". Part of maintaining
Professional Discipline in the Creative Economy is the ability
to say "no".

"No" in the Creative Economy is always carefully considered,
is actually a "yes" to something else,
is not a "no" to the person, but a "no" to the request.

"No" is an expression of
professional boundaries,
not a rejection of
professional relationships.

"No" is your first line of defense against professional,
creative, and personal burnout.

There is nothing more
professional than a
well-earned "no".

Thoughts on Communal Discipline

This is "together discipline". These are the patterns we develop as a group, a tribe, a community.

Keep these in mind:

Friends don't let friends slack off.

Hold each other accountable.

Expect greatness.

Demand excellence.

Success is not an accident.

Use your love to encourage others, not to enable them.

Groups move together.

Office Space

89.7% of all workplace complaints have to do with a coworker's lack of discipline: missing deadlines, arriving late, poor focus, and failing to execute in a timely manner.

The other 11.3% of complaints have to do with workplace conditions and vending machine selection.

I made up those stats, btw.

Seems legit.

Discipline
determines
your
reputation.

Those are the voices of the Creative Economy.

You have to listen closely to hear them.

These voices will never yell.

They will only whisper.

In today's world, this whisper may show up in many forms:

A meme
A supportive voice from your past
A lyric in a song
An Instagram post
A blog post
A sermon
That thing your mother
always told you that you thought was dumb. (Maybe she was right.)
A stranger's t-shirt
A book about career
A poster in a coffee shop
A fortune cookie

Listen closely and keep your eyes open.

Creativity will use
creative ways
to reach you.

Sometimes Creative
Economy Voices
are hard to hear.

But, like all voices, they
come from somewhere.

They're built on something.
They come from somewhere.

They're resting on a foundation.

Here is the foundation for
the Creative Economy

Cause

Community

Practice

Offering

When you build your career upon this foundation, creative voices are easier to hear.

Inspiration is the natural result of a well- supported artist.

Cause

Why?

Because

Why?

Cause

Why?

Just Cause

How?

Be Cause

A Cause is your

Why
Purpose
Reason
Mojo
Driving force
Energy
Calling

It's the thing that pulls you through the darkness,
the difficult times, and roots you in meaning.

It's the thing you will spend your life in service to.

It is the foundation upon
which you build
your career.

If a meal is only as good as its ingredients, then a
career is only as good as its cause.

If a home is only as strong as its foundation, then a career is
only as strong as its cause.

If the quality of a wine is determined by the quality of the soil,
then the quality of the career is determined by the quality of
the cause.

Wine.

Yummm..

Wine.

I love wine.

Why?

Just, cause.

duh.

Imagine a leaf blowing in the wind. Moving in circles, up and down, round and round.

At the mercy of the wind, free to move only where the wind takes it.

When the wind blows, it moves. When the wind is still, it stays waiting on the ground waiting for the next gust.

How romantic.

But a leaf in the wind cannot decide where it goes. A leaf in the wind is always at the mercy of the breeze. It never chooses, isn't accountable, and never lands where it wants to land.

It has no cause.

Life is happening to the leaf, but the leaf cannot make life happen.

Do not be a leaf blowing in the wind.

It's not hard to convince people that cause is important...

Most people agree with me.

Most people know how important it is.

Most people get it.

But, most people don't know how to find it.

So, they never find it.

They burn out.

They stop trying.

They become leaves blowing in the wind.

Then blame the wind for not taking them where they dreamed of going.

Sound familiar?

I hope not.

Consider

these

three

things

when

defining

your

cause:

It's not about you.

Your cause cannot be rooted in a me-first perspective.

Cause should be rooted in an others-oriented perspective.

For example, "to get rich" is not a cause. But, "to get rich, so I can end homelessness" might be.

We always do more for others than for ourselves.

It's the journey of
every hero.

It's not something you do, it's something you live.

Your cause is not something
for you to simply achieve.

Cause is the fuel that propels your journey, not the result
of the journey itself.

It's not a goal to be completed, measured, or evaluated.

It is the current that moves through you and is reflected
in everything you do.

If it can be achieved, it's too small to be your cause.

A cause that will take you into tomorrow is probably something that pisses you off today.

What bothers you?

Are you concerned with social injustice, poverty, or homelessness?

What keeps you up at night?

What do you avoid talking about at polite dinner parties?

Issues that pain your heart are issues you are uniquely qualified to address. That's where you'll find your cause.

(Remember when I talked about the difference between anger as a response, and a reaction? This is what I was talking about.)

Achieving your dreams
will never satisfy you,
never make you whole.

There will always be more.
There will always be another role
another show
another job
another check.

But, living your Cause
your purpose
your calling
will.

Community

When you look to the people around you,
are you able to
say this:

"Knowing who you are today, and who you are determined to become tomorrow, I would rather lose with you than win with anyone else."

If you can say that about the people you surround yourself with, then the people you surround yourself with are your

Community.

Someone once said:

"You are the average of the 5 people closest to you."

Someone said that.

But, it doesn't mean it's true.

The person who said this did not understand community.

Keep reading...I'll explain.

Let's play a game!

Community or Clique!

I'll give you a description, and you tell me if it's a community or a clique.

Ready?!

Here we go!

Imagine a group of people who hang out all the time. They all believe that chocolate milk is the best thing EVER! They love the velvety texture, the sugary goodness, and the refreshing aftertaste. They wear the same clothes, drink Chocolate Milk at the same milk bars, and always talk about Chocolate Milk. They all dream of a day when Chocolate Milk will be deemed the national drink of the United States. They are all friends, spend most of their day together, and even date each other. Their love for Chocolate Milk has brought them together and nothing will separate them. One day, someone who loves Orange Juice tries to join their group. Immediately, the members of the Chocolate Milk group tell the Orange Juice lover that, "we respect your preference for Orange Juice, but you should find an Orange Juice group. It just wouldn't make sense for you to join our group. We all think the same way, like the same things, and have the same dreams. So, if you really wanted to join our group, you'd have to be more like us."

Now...

Imagine a group of people who are trying to feed every hungry person in the world. They meet regularly to work together, to feed the hungry, and to organize their efforts. Some of the people in the group are friends. They hang out together, they date each other, and they vacation together. Other members are not friends. They never see each other outside of a group function, they have friends outside of the group, and spend a lot of time with other friends. Some members of the group are very conservative, some members are very liberal. Some members of the group are very religious, and others are atheists. A few members of the group dress the same way. They wear skinny jeans, and shaman hats. Others wear pleated pants and sandals with socks. One day a new person wants to join the group. This person has never fed a hungry person, but has a newly discovered passion for feeding homeless children. This new person is from out of town and does not dress like anyone else, does not think like anyone else, and feels lost in a new city. The members of the group say, "Nice to meet you. We're excited to have you join our cause, and look forward to helping you feed homeless children. Welcome home."

Which one is a community and which one is a clique?

Is it obvious?

If you've made it this far into this book, it should be obvious.

The first group, the Chocolate Milk group, is a clique.

The second group, the Feed the Hungry group, is a community.

Here's why:

A true community inspires ACCEPTANCE, not CONFORMITY.

It is a place where the person is allowed to be themselves even as they are included within the larger group. It is a place where the outsider can feel both included and unpressured to conform.

In the first group, the Chocolate Milk lovers required the Orange Juice lover to conform to their standards.

If you must conform in order
to be accepted,
you are not
in community.

Community is rooted in Like-Heartedness, not Like-Mindedness.

In the Feed the Hungry Group, the people were unified by a cause in their hearts, not an idea in their minds.

When a group of people are united by cause, diversity of thought becomes a strength, not a liability.

People can
have different opinions about big things like politics, religion, and economics, and still be driven by the same cause.

There is less distance between
hearts than between minds.

Community is not divided by opposing ideas because it is not defined by aligned ideas.

Community is not necessarily a group of friends.

Sure. People in community can be friends. But, it's not a requirement or a sign of a healthy community.

Don't force friendships, and don't mistake a group of friends for a community.

In the Chocolate Milk group, everyone was friends. Friends have a tendency not to challenge each other, or hold each other accountable. Friends have a tendency to let each other "get away with it."

That ain't cool.

A community always challenges its members to live up to their greatness, not down to their mediocrity.

In community, boundaries are not points of division, but points of contact.

In a clique, the group uses boundaries to divide themselves from others. Communities have boundaries also, but the boundaries are not used to divide. They are used to make contact.

Have you ever seen two communities work together to create something they could not create alone? Imagine if our Feed the Hungry group partnered with a Shelter the Homeless group. Together they fed and sheltered thousands of people. Two communities maintaining their unique causes and strengths maintaining their boundaries but working together to make more happen. When a community maintains the integrity of its cause, and works together with another community, boundaries become points of contact, not points of division.

Communities are living things.

They grow, they change, and, without nurturing, they can die.

To keep a community thriving you must

Believe in

Invest In

and

Celebrate

the people in your community.

Believe In

Believing in people is hard.

People will let you down. They will lie to you. They will always make things difficult.

Even in
(especially in)
Communities

Let's face it communities would be much easier if people weren't involved.

A community of one would have less conflict than a community of many.

Less conflict, but less growth.

Easier is not always better.

Belief in community is not
rooted in who someone is today

but

Who they are working to become.

You must believe in their journey.

Believe in the path they are setting for themselves.

See the members of your community through the lens of who
they are
Becoming.

Who are they becoming?

Who are you becoming?

That's what you believe in.

Invest In

Communities thrive on engagement.

Get involved.

Stay involved.

Engagement is the natural result of a deep belief in a group of people.

Offer to help,
be the first to arrive,
take out the trash,
randomly call someone to congratulate them.

The level of your investment is measured in the dedication of your involvement.

Get involved.

Make the investment.

Like all investments,

it's going to cost you something.

Time
Attention
Effort
Patience
Love

But, unlike some investments, when you invest in people there
is always a return.

Always.

Yes, always.

Even if it takes a while.

There is always a

return.

Never underestimate the value of your investment.

When you invest in someone, you are saying:

"I believe in you. I know what you are capable of doing, and I admire your willingness to do it."

When you invest in someone, you are saying:

"I know this is hard, but you're not alone! Keep going!"

You may offer someone an opportunity, your time, some money, or just a simple word of encouragement.

It doesn't matter

Even the smallest investment can be the difference in someone's career.

Celebrate

The ability for members of a community to genuinely celebrate the victories of other members is one of the most re-
vealing measures of a community's health.

Personal Victories

Professional Victories

Communal Victories

No matter how small,
no matter how big,

when you celebrate the victory,

you celebrate
the community.

Celebration and
jealousy cannot
exist in the
same space

There are three types of celebration:

Private celebrations

Public celebrations

Secret celebrations

Private Celebrations

happen when you are one-on-one with the person you are celebrating.

You look them in the eye, you shake their hand, or you give them a high five.

This is when you give them a big hug, tell them how proud of them you are, and how honored you are to be in their community.

Private celebrations are genuine, meaningful, and are a reflection of your dedication to the individual.

These moments matter.

Use them well.

Public Celebrations

happen when someone's victory is acknowledged in front of the
community.

This is when you invite the victor to tell their story, to share
their good news, and to be celebrated in front of everyone.

This is when you clap, you cheer, and you make a lot of noise.

Honoring someone in front of their peers is a humbling
experience for everyone.

Public celebrations are genuine, meaningful, and are a
reflection of the humility of the community.

These moments matter.

Use them well.

Secret Celebrations

happen when members of the community brag about someone behind their back. It's like gossip, except you're saying good things about them.

It might sound like this:

"Did you hear about Emma?! She just booked her dream job!

"That's incredible! She deserves all the success in the world."

These are the best types of celebrations.

The. Best.

Secret celebrations are genuine, meaningful, and are a reflection of the strength of the community.

These moments matter.

Use them often.

By the way...

Bragging about someone
behind their back is the opposite of gossip.

If you want to end a cycle of gossip,
start bragging about people.

All it will do is change your
world.

That's all.

NBD.

If all this celebrating
sounds like
blowing
smoke.

I understand.

But, trust me, it's not blowing smoke.

It's fanning flames.

In community,

meaning comes
from a shared past,

moments come
from a shared present,

momentum comes
from a shared future.

So, you see, you are not the average
of the people you surround
yourself with.

You are the sum

Strength
Talent
Forgiveness
Determination
Network
Resource
Support
Creativity...

of your community.

*a note on Community.

Communities are living organisms, and not everyone with you today will be with you tomorrow.

Your tribe will grow as you grow, and not everyone is capable of going on the journey you are on. A person committed to self-discovery and improvement will lose some people along the way. Not everyone grows at the same pace, not everyone is strong enough, and few have the courage it takes to live a life of purpose in a creative economy.

It's ok.

Good people choose different paths.

Let them.

Priorities shift, and different choices must be made.

Not everyone will be capable of going where you are going.

Practice

What if I told you that most
people approach their acting career
like a battle they
cannot win.

No matter the victories,
no matter the ladder they climb,

there is always more to achieve,
always another step on the ladder,

there is always someone above them,
someone who looks down on them,

there is always...something.

For them,
career is a war,
and every day is a battle.

And every day,
no matter what happens,
they lose.

Guess what?

It doesn't have to be this way.

Instead of thinking about your acting career as a battle you cannot win, think of it as a pursuit you cannot lose.

Your acting career is not a thing to be achieved.

Not a skill to be mastered.

Not a life spent burdened with judgment, evaluations, and auditions.

It is not a job to be executed,

it is a
practice

to be lived.

If you want a life-long journey of

growth,
creativity,
artistry,
success,
and
fulfillment,

you must come to see your
acting career as a
Practice.

A never-ending process that
cannot be right or wrong,
mastered or completed.

Nothing to gain,
nothing to lose.

I know.
I know.

But what about results?

Are you really telling me that there is no WRONG way to live my acting career?

Yep.

But, you don't know my agent.

You're right.

You don't know my day job.

You're right.

You don't know the pressure I'm under.

You're right.

If I don't prepare, if I don't audition, if I don't book the job, I can't pay my rent.

You're right.

Practice is not a replacement for accountability.

Practice is not a substitute for results.

Practice does not give you permission to suck.

Practice frees you to be excellent

Superior

Outrageous

Magnificent

Stupendous

and

Incredible

in your career.

Neither is Practice the repetition of an activity.

It's not about doing something over and over and over and
over and over
and over and over and over and over.

There is a difference between having TO practice,
and being IN practice.

Practice is a mindset, a perspective, and an approach.

Practice is not a
WHAT you do.

Practice is a
HOW you do.

Practice defines the relationship you have towards the things you do.

Do you do things to master them, to get them right, or to finish them?

If so, it is not a practice.

It's a task,
or a job,
or a chore.

But, as you do things, if you learn from them, investigate them,
and enjoy them,
you are in Practice.

A job is a series of
8 hour tasks
40 hours a week
160 hours a month
2000 hours a year.

A Practice is a continuous path
of growth,

and it is never over.

It's a full time,
even on the weekend,
even on holiday's,
even at 6pm,

perspective

on your career,
and the things you make,
and the people you affect,
and the lives you touch,
and the relationships you love.

If you think about it:

Yoga is a practice. It can never be mastered, finished, or perfected.

Law is a practice. It can never be mastered, finished, or perfected.

Medicine is a practice. It can never be mastered, finished, or perfected.

Acting is a practice. It can never be mastered, finished, or perfected.

Cooking is a practice. It can never be mastered, finished, or perfected.

Business is a practice. It can never be mastered, finished, or perfected.

Parenting is a practice. It can never be mastered, finished, or perfected.

Marriage is a practice. It can never be mastered, finished, or perfected.

Bartending is a practice. It can never be mastered, finished, or perfected.

Accounting is a practice. It can never be mastered, finished, or perfected.

Law enforcement is a practice. It can never be mastered, finished, or perfected.

Craft Brewing is a practice. It can never be mastered, finished, or perfected.

Carpentry is a practice. It can never be mastered, finished, or perfected.

Farming is a practice. It can never be mastered, finished, or perfected.

Grand-mothering is a practice. It can never be mastered, finished, or perfected.

And...

You are a practice. You can never be mastered, finished, or perfected.

If you think something
can be mastered,
you've obviously
never met
a

master.

A practice continues
to develop the

person

long after the skill is

acquired.

A practice celebrates
the depth of

process

over the height of

product.

A practice cannot be quantified in results.

Money
Points
Likes
Views
Handshakes
Reviews
Customers
Sales
Auditions
Fans
Articles...

...are side effects.

They come
and go.

But a practice remains.

Freedom in practice

and

addiction to results

cannot exist at the same time.

So, instead

go for the going,
sing for the singing,
kiss for the kissing,

hold for the holding,
smile for the smiling,
dance for the dancing,

make for the making,
cook for the cooking,
give for the giving,

act for the acting.

Joyful doing is result enough.

Practice is not about getting it right;
it's about getting it true.

It's not about being faultless;
it's about being false less.

Even in
(especially in)
your acting career.

Practice is not
afraid of mistakes.

Practice values
wisdom,

and mistakes
are the
source of wisdom.

So, practice is not
afraid of mistakes.

Your life is long enough to
withstand mistakes.

So is your
acting career.

Mistakes in your acting career
are like commas in a paragraph—
they make you pause,
but they are not
the end
of the
sentence.

Practice is the perspective
that allows you to keep writing
the pages of your
your career.

Practice allows for

the pursuit of excellence

without the pitfall of perfectionism.

Excellence is a standard for future performance, and drives all great artists.

Perfectionism is a condemnation of past performance, and stalls all great artists.

Practice breeds excellence
not perfectionism.

You cannot be in practice and
be a perfectionist
at the same time.

Your acting career is a practice.

To see it any other way
is to prepare yourself
for a life of
needless
suffering.

So...

Don't do that.

Offering

Ok.

This is the part you've been waiting for.

This is the part where I tell you what to do with your new understanding of the Creative Economy.

This is the part where we talk about the day-to-day administration of your Acting career.

This is when we talk about the WHAT.

The DOING.

There are lots of books, articles, and lists that also talk about an actor's career administration.

Keep reading.

I promise this is different.

It's easy to talk about the Creative Economy.

It's easy to philosophize,
to dream,
to agree with good ideas.

It's easy to nod your head and take notes when you get inspired.

It's easy to believe in the Creative Economy.

It's a good idea. A nice thought.

And seems cool.

But, if what you believe in
doesn't change the way you live,
you don't really believe
in it.

It's easy to keep a Creative Economy perspective when everything is going well.

When you're booking work,
when you love your agent,
when you're making money,
when you're auditioning a lot,
when all your community is on fire,
when your time management is efficient.

But, it's much harder to keep a Creative Economy perspective when everything sucks.

When you aren't booking work,
when your day job is draining,
when your agent drops you,
when your community dissolves,
when you feel bitter,
when you want to quit.

But this is when it matters most.

This industry will let you down. It is inconsistent, unpredictable, and overwhelming.

People lie, cheat, and steal.

And, sometimes they are rewarded for that.

But,

it's like that for everyone.

Everyone.

It's not about you.

It's not against you.

It's never personal.

It's not a reflection on you.

It's a reflection on the industry.

The way you approach your career
must be strong enough to shoulder
the weakness of the industry...

...not compensate for it.

Yes, this is going to be hard.

This is going to take a while.

Yes, this is unpredictable.

Things will happen that you never expected, envisioned, or planned for.

And, that can be overwhelming.

But the only solution
to overwhelming circumstances,
is overwhelming determination.

Mt. Everest didn't shrink for the people who climbed it.

You can do this.

I promise.

You can do this.

Here's how.

I'm going to give you three things to do EVERY DAY that will help you build the career you want without losing the person you want to become.

As you do these things, continue to listen for the whispers of

Patience
Hope
Generosity
Discipline.

Sometimes they will be hard to hear.

There will be times when you won't want to listen. You'll question, roll your eyes, lose hope, and get frustrated.

Be careful.

The voices of Fear, Doubt, Greed, and Anger are loud.

But, remember, the loudest voice isn't always the truth.

As you work with these three things remember,

you must continue to

trust your cause,
engage your community,
and remain in practice.

It will be easy for Entitlement, Obligation, Tasks, and Individualism to creep their way into the day-to-day management of your acting career.

But don't be afraid of these Corporate Voices.

There will be conflict.

Conflict is the material of a creative life.

It sharpens you, strengthens you,

and keeps you focused.

Just keep going

Ok, here are the three things you must do every day to manage your acting career in a Creative Economy.

1. Reach In

2. Reach Out

3. Reach To

Reach In

Everything we create is an EXPANSION of who we are. Every word we speak, every thought we write, every feeling we express, is an expansion of an inner truth.

That means everything you need for this career, you already have.

This is easy to forget, so you have to reach deep inside yourself.

You have to sharpen the ax,
oil the machine,
remove the weeds.

You have to remind yourself
of the story of who you are.

You have to reflect.
The first, and most significant, element of managing a day-to-day career as an actor, is Reaching In.

The Windmill and the Wind

There once was a young windmill sitting alone on top of a hill above a small town.

Every day, the windmill would spin and spin and spin. He would spin at the slightest breeze, and he would spin at the strongest gust.

And every day, the people in the town would wave to the windmill thanking him for making the energy they need to light their lights and cool their homes.

He was a happy windmill.

And it was a very happy town.

Then, one day the windmill saw a storm on the horizon, so he braced himself for the rain and the wind.

Suddenly, with a loud BANG, the storm arrived. The windmill began to turn faster than he ever turned before. As he spun, the rain seeped into the gears, deep into the joints of his arms.

For three days, the storm raged.

For three days, the windmill spun at a mighty pace. And for three days, rainwater dripped into his gears and onto the joints of his arms.

The people smiled as they watched the windmill turning. For they knew it was creating more energy for them to enjoy.

Finally, the storm passed and the windmill slowed down.

The townspeople, having plenty of energy from the storm, began to ignore the windmill. They stopped waving to the windmill. Stopped thanking him for working so hard.

Alone, and on top of the hill, the windmill sat still. No longer spinning.

For weeks, the windmill did not turn. For weeks, no one waved to him, or thanked him, or appreciated him.

Then one day, the townspeople ran out of energy. Their lights began to go off, and their houses could not be cooled. It was dark, hot, and the town had no power.

So, they began to look at the lonely windmill on top of the hill.

Enraged they screamed,

"Why are you not spinning?!"
"Turn!" They demanded.

"We need energy! You have to spin!!" They pleaded.

The windmill listened alone and afraid. He loved the townspeople and he was ashamed that he was not spinning.

Just then, a strong breeze came through the sky. Trees were bending in the wind, leaves were scattered in the air, and hats flew off heads.

The townspeople celebrated, knowing the windmill would turn again and they would have energy.

But, even in the wind, the windmill stood still.

"There is a breeze! Why won't you turn?!" They asked.

"You are doing this on purpose!" They accused.

"You are worthless if you cannot do your job!" They shamed.

Suddenly, the windmill responded, cursing the wind.

"I do not feel a breeze. There is no breeze to move my arms. I see others moving in the wind, but I cannot feel it myself. If only the wind would blow for me!!"
The townspeople responded,
"Why can't you feel the breeze? It's there!! We feel it, we see it, it's all around you!"

The windmill refused to believe the wind was blowing, so he tried to spin himself. He tried to force his arms to move.

He pushed and pushed and pushed, but his arms would not move. He gave everything he had to move his arms, and still they would not budge.

Overcome with failure, exhausted, embarrassed, and angry at the wind, he began to cry tears of oil.

At this, the townspeople pointed and laughed.

"The windmill is crying! He cannot spin, so he is crying!"

But, as his oily tears began to drip into his arm joints, he could feel his arms begin to move.
When his tears had washed fully into his arm joints and gears, he noticed a brown residue dripping off his arms.

"What is that?" He wondered.

The more he cried, the more the brown residue dripped off his arms, the more his arms began to move in the wind.

Suddenly, he could feel the breeze!! It was there! It was all around him!

Then he heard the voice of a young girl echo through the hills.

"It's ok to cry, gentle windmill. You have survived a giant storm. You were exhausted, and the rain from the storm rusted your joints. Keep crying, and you will spin again. The oil in your tears is melting away the rust in your gears."

Like a dam bursting, the windmill wept. And as he wept, the oil in his tears dissolved away the rust. Suddenly, his arms began to turn in the breeze, and the townspeople's lights began to flicker on.

The little girl was right.

As he spun and spun, the windmill apologized to the wind.

It was only through his tears that he realized he had confused dying wind for drying oil.

As the townspeople reveled in their celebrations, they looked to the windmill and said,

"From now on, we vow to dry and oil your gears after a storm. You are too important to us, and we will help take care of the things that make you spin."

The windmill, smiling a giant windmill-sized smile, looked at the townspeople and said,

"You are important to me, too. From now on, I promise to never blame the wind for my rusted joints."

Just then, the wind came rushing down the hill and through the town. Leaves swirled, hats flew, trees danced

And the windmill spun.

Reaching In is the process of continuous inspiration.

It's going inside yourself to clean out the rust, to shake off the cobwebs, and to reignite the fire.

It's anything that shines a light into the dark forgotten corners of your heart, and reminds you why you started this whole thing to begin with.

It's the process of nurturing your creativity in creative ways.

It's like exercise for your soul.

And you have to do it.

Every day.

Reaching In roots your career in the most fertile ground possible,

you.

So,

stop listening to the echo,

stop admiring the reflections.

Who cares about the smoke,
take care of the fire.

You are the cause,
not the effect.

You are the source
of your career.

You are where
it all begins.

Reaching in often begins with this question:

Where do I go to find
my strength?

Do you:
Read books that challenge you
Watch films that inspire you
Pray
Journal
Spend time dreaming about your future (you should do this
more often, btw)
Turn off your phone, take off your watch, and go for a walk
Listen to music
Paint, Dance, Surf
Spend time with people you miss, See a play, Read a play,
Make time for reflection

Anything you do that makes you feel more inspired, challenged, stronger, purpose filled, or creative qualifies as
Reaching in.

Reaching In is often overlooked. When we feel crunched for time, we sacrifice the things we deem less urgent, or less pressing. It's important to develop a strategy around your Reaching In.

Some forms of Reaching In are daily practices:
Morning coffee, exercise,
meditation.

Others are weekly practices:
Religious services, date nights
basketball league.

Others are quarterly practices:
Weekend getaways, connecting with old friends, running a 5K.

Others are annual practices:
Meditation retreat, beach vacation,
running a triathlon.

Reaching In takes different forms for different people. All is intended to melt away the rust so you can turn with the wind.

Sometimes this career will seem like you are jumping from one crisis to another.

Solving problems that cause other problems that create new problems.

And it's all you can do to make it through the day, one day at a time.

This is why you Reach In.

If you don't know who you are,
and remind yourself of who you are,
and remember the story of who you are,
and keep the fire lit inside,

you will be shaped by your circumstances.

If the world inside you is not alive,
you'll be shaped by the
world outside
you.

Create your circumstances,
don't let them create you.

Reaching In as Rest.

Actors, too often we forget to rest. Or we misunderstand rest, so we do things we think will restore us, but we end up exhausted.

For rest to be truly effective, it needs to be coupled with the feeling that you are satisfied with where you are and can now restore. Many actors are never satisfied with where they are, and so refuse to rest. We are addicted to "doing", so "being" is a difficult task.

But, fatigue is not a status symbol.

Rest is an integral part of maintaining a career in a Creative Economy, and it's an important part of Reaching In.

Rest is short for Restoration. When we rest, we should feel restored. Sleep is certainly a form of rest, but rest can be woven into our work.

Rest can be active. Rest does not necessarily mean "do nothing".

Rest is a Choice.

The first thing we must realize is that rest is a choice.
If you never choose to rest, you are telling yourself that
you are not in control of your work.

You have enslaved yourself to your career,
and are no longer in practice.

You have given away the very freedom that is the source of
your creativity.

The inability to rest is the first sign of an unhealthy
relationship to your work.

Rest Accelerates Progress.

When we Reach In and rest, we take the time we need to
sharpen the ax.

This makes cutting down the tree much easier.

It may feel counterintuitive, but Reaching In accelerates
progress and
makes us more
productive.

3 Types of Rest

Rest is a big word, and sometimes it seems overwhelming, so we never approach it.

But, rest takes on many forms and can be experienced in many ways.

1. Mix-It-Up Rest. Anytime we break a routine, drop a habit, or mix our day up, it can be restorative. Try driving a new way to work, or waking up at an earlier time, or changing your morning routine. Embracing the new within the mundane is restorative and can be considered rest.

2. Clear-Your-Mind Rest. This is when you spend the time in true solitude. This is contemplative rest. This is when you provide space for yourself to reflect on your dreams, your past, and your future. This is when you take quiet time, and listen to the creative voices that are always whispering to you.

3. Power-Down Rest. This is when you just sit on your couch and do nothing! Yes, there is a time for that. Maybe you watch TV, play video games, or just take a nap. When the un-planned is allowed to remain unplanned, it can be restorative.

Defining success.

As you Reach In, listen closely for your personal definition of success.

There are limitless versions of successful careers in

Movies
TV
Children's Theatre
Broadway
Immersive Theatre
Shakespeare in Prison Programs
Improv
High School Theatre Programs
Community Theatre
Commercials
Musical Theatre
Regional Theatre
Voice Over

...to name a few

Don't let anyone define success for you. Reach In, listen deeply, and
define it for yourself.

As you grow in your career, your definition of success may change.

That's ok!

Success in a Creative Economy
is an evolving, growing, and dynamic condition.

It is not static.

As we grow and mature, our priorities shift. Our family, finances, faith, fitness, and friendships may shift.

That's ok.

Let them.

Measure your success across all areas of your life, because in a Creative Economy, it's all connected. Success in my relationships leads to success in my art which leads to success in my career.

By taking care of one, you take care of it all.
It is through Reaching In, that you discover the truest version of personal success.

Every aspect of your career management must be aligned
with this definition of success.
You must always return to it and ask,

"Am I still on that path? Do I still value that definition of
success? Are the choices I make today pointing towards the
success I want to achieve tomorrow?"

When you feel your actions are aligned with your definition of
success,
you must work tirelessly and optimistically to achieve it.

Because...

if you don't work to achieve your version of success, someone
will hire
you to achieve theirs.

Reach Out

This is the stuff everyone talks about. This is the stuff you probably know to do...but aren't doing.

This is where the "self-management for actors" stuff lives. The "top ten things you should be doing for your career" stuff lives. The "my acting teacher told me to do this" stuff lives.

This is where that stuff lives, but in the Creative Economy, that stuff lives very differently.

Keep reading.

Reaching Out is about sharing yourself with the world. It's about sharing your work with the world.

It's how you go from where you are to where you want to be.

Careful. The Corporate Voices will work hard to throw you off course.

Doubt
Greed
Anger
Fear

will work hard to convince you that you aren't progressing fast enough.

They will frustrated you.

They will make you unprofessional.

They will make you desperate.

And, desperation killed more careers than apathy ever did.

Time.

You have 168 hours in week.

Let's say you sleep for 8 hours a day, which is 56 hours a week.

That leaves you with 112 waking hours a week.

Let's pretend you have a full-time job at 40 hours a week.

You would still have 72 hours left to manage your acting career.

Let's say you spend 40 hours a week managing your acting career, you would still have 32 hours left to do

whatever. you. wanted.

Are you spending 40 hours a week on your career?

If not, where is all your time going?

Time is like money,
you should determine
where it goes.

Account for every hour.

Use them wisely.

Time is opportunity.

And people, Facebook, Instagram, coffee, Snapchat, YouTube,
TV,
and about 2 million other things
want to steal it from you.

Don't let them.

Un-addict yourself from
things that steal your opportunities.

If you don't have a day planner
get one.

Now.

Put the book down,

and go get a planner.

Then, use it.

Seriously.

Yes, you can use your
phone calendar.

Too many actors want the benefits of a full-time acting career without dedicating the time to a full-time career.

There are no quick fixes.

There are no get-rich-quick schemes.

There is no magic teacher,

Agent
Manager
Casting Director
Producer
Director

that will get you where you want to go.

This career takes time.

This is a 10-year plan...
with a 60-year contingency

if you're lucky.

(This is why patience matters.)

Here's how you might spend your time in a Creative Economy:

Let's assume you have a full-time, 40-hour-a-week survival job.

You have 72 hrs left to build your acting career.

Of the 72 hrs, let's use 40 of them.

That means you have 40 hours to divide among the three career management principles

Reach In
Reach Out
Reach To

That's about 13 hrs every week for each one.

For 52 weeks a year. For 60 more years.
If you do this from the Creative Economy, I promise you will build the career you want without losing the person you are.

The Day Job Dilemma

Your day job is important.

Stop complaining about it.

Treat your day job like an ANGEL INVESTOR for your dream job.

Your day job employer is paying you and will never ask for that money back.

If you invest that money into your acting career, your employer becomes your investor.

Isn't that awesome.

Be recklessly grateful
for every job
you have.

The Myth of Self-Promotion

Many actors hate to "promote" themselves, hate to "sell" themselves.

But in a Creative Economy, you don't need to "sell" yourself to elevate your acting career.

When we "promote" and "sell" ourselves, we are giving our power to other people.

We are asking them to raise us above what we are capable of doing for ourselves.

"Self-Promotion" asks people to give you value, but does not provide value for other people.

That's why it feels gross. That's why it feels icky. That's why you hate doing it.

Cause you're a good person
and don't want to feel like an
asshole.

But, when we offer
ourselves to others
we bring them value.

Share yourself.

Don't promote yourself.

Offer your work to the world.

Offer it well.

Offer it often.

Set your heart on fire

And they will come to read

by your light.

Consider everything you
create

as good news

as worthy

as unique

as beautiful

and you will
find joy in offering it
to the world

There are many ways to
share your work with the world. But it all begins with your
Practice your passion and interest in the work.

Are you doing work you're interested in doing, or are you
doing work to be interesting? The only way to be interesting
is to be interested in what you are doing.

Do a

Play
Short film
Staged reading
Immersive Theatre Piece

because you believe in
the people,
the project,
and the process.

Then, you'll find sharing
it with the world is a
natural result of your
belief in the work.

Here are a few examples of Reaching Out, of sharing your work with the world:

Make posters, make postcards, email friends, call friends
social media posts, street corner demonstrations, email reviewers,
reach out to a retirement home and offer them discounted tickets,
offer a talkback to a local high school,
dress up like a Newsie from the 1920's and hand out flyers about your show,
host a dream party and invite friends to come eat, drink, and talk about the show,
recruit everyone you know and ask them to tell one person about the show,
cold email people in the industry, attach your work, and ask them to read/watch it, contact like-caused institutions and invite them to a special screening of your film...

The same creativity you engaged to make your project is the same creativity it will take to
share it.

The Social Media of It All

Yes. Social media is an important way to Reach Out in the Creative Economy.

You need to have a presence, and that presence needs to be consistent and curated.

But, be careful.

Nothing attracts the pitfalls of a Corporate Economy better than social media.

Social media is a giant petri dish that grows Doubt, Greed, Fear, and Anger
at alarming rates.

But, it can also be the largest platform to share the fruit of your Patience, Hope, Generosity, and Discipline.

Here are some principles for managing your social media presence as you Reach Out in a Creative Economy.

The McValue Meal Principle.
Your Social Media is only as valuable as the value it provides others. This means that the majority of your posts need to provide value to the people who see it. Every post is an

offering that makes them feel something or think something. Their time is limited, your profile should not be a waste of their time. Every post should make someone's day better.

The Back Scratchers Principle.

Reciprocity is king. You must earn the right to make an "ask" on social media. Before you use Instagram to ask people to see your film, you should have already given them something of value. It is through offering value that you establish relationships and reciprocity on Social Media. So, follow the 4 to 1 rule. You must post 4 offerings for every request you make. If your audience finds value in your profile, then they will respond when you Reach Out to share your work. Scratch my back, and I'll want to scratch yours.

The Way You Make Me Feel Principle

Value creates influencers, likes' do not. Do not associate the quality of your influence with the number of likes you receive. Likes do not represent quality. If your social media presence does not provide a valuable experience to others, you have no influence over them.

The Loudest Voice Isn't Always the Truth Principle

Stop believing that the number of followers and percentage of engagement will make you more hirable. It's not true. This myth originated because producers believed that "number of followers" would influence the number of tickets sold. So,

there was an effort to cast actors with large social media followings to convince investors that the cast had monetary value based on their social media influence. They were wrong. Very wrong. The numbers have proven that quantity of followers does not indicate quantity of tickets sold. It turns out that the psychological impulse to like" or follow' an actor is not the same thing that causes someone to actually spend money to see a film they're in. And, because the quantity of followers is not an indicator of the quality of the actor, an actor's social media profile has zero bearing on the success of a film, and therefore, on their ability to be cast.
READ THIS AGAIN.

<u>The "Everything has a Price" Principle</u>
Likes, followers, and engagement can all be purchased. Google it. If your agent still believes you need more followers, go buy some. Who cares. It's all a joke anyway. Just stop spending more time on your social media than on your work.

Here's the deal.

Artists with truly engaged fans, fans that are loyal, fans that will buy tickets, come to shows, and support their work, developed their **work** before they developed their **social media.**

In a Creative Economy, Social media is an important vehicle for Reaching Out to share your work.

But, do not confuse it for
the work.

Look at your Instagram account.

How many of your
first 12 photos
are selfies?

0-3: You're probably a cool mom.

4-7: Ok, we get it. You're pretty.

8-11: You might want to talk to someone

12: Call your mother. She loves you. Don't forget that.
You are lovable.
You are worthy.

Your Brand

Your brand is not a logo.
Your brand is not a website.
Your brand is not a filter.
Your brand is not a genre.
Your brand is not a character type.
Your brand is not a charity.
Your brand is not a style.
Your brand is not your story.

Your brand is the feeling people have when they engage with you.

When you Reach Out, do they feel obligated, or do they see an opportunity?

When you Reach Out, do they see an expert actor, or an expert marketer?

Your brand is the feeling people have after they have experienced your work, your person, and your presence.

Actors.

Stop branding yourself.

Start being yourself.

Your Team

You cannot do this on your own. You will need a professional team. Agents, managers, lawyers, and PR reps will help you as you navigate the industry.

Here are some ways to approach getting, keeping, and motivating your team in the Creative Economy.

Put yourself in an agent's shoes. Do you understand their job? Do you understand the pain points, frustrations, and difficulties of their job?

Agents spend their days reading breakdowns, submitting clients,
pitching clients,
developing relationships,
negotiating on behalf of clients,
eating lunch at their desks,
arriving early
and staying late.

You must make their lives easier, not more difficult.

You must be a solution for them, not a problem.

Understand who they are as people,
and you will understand
the person they are
looking for.

The best way to be a solution for an agent is to make yourself easy for them to pitch. The best way to make yourself easy to pitch is to be working.

Work on anything.

A play.
A short film.
A sketch comedy show.

A working actor is easier to pitch than a stagnant actor.

If you want to sign with an agent, you must be, or appear to be, moving forward without them.

Then, when you reach out to them, you are inviting them to join your journey, not begging for representation.

It is your job to create the momentum.

It's their job to accelerate it.

<u>These are the nuts and bolts of getting an agent or manager.</u>

Get a headshot.
Build a resume. Shoot a reel.
Make content.
Do plays. Do stand-up comedy.
Do sketch comedy.
Do anything.

Let them know about it, and invite them.

Email them with your original content attached.
Send them a postcard.

(Do not call them)

Print your headshot, staple your resume on the back, write a clever cover letter, buy some envelopes, buy stamps, and mail a hard copy to every agent you want to work with.

Do this for a year, at least.

One of the most effective ways to get an agent is to be introduced.

Ask people in your community for a reference.

But, do this mindfully.

As a rule, you can ask for this kind of reference twice every 3 years. Use it wisely.

Ask someone in your community who is familiar with your work, who loves your work, and who has a good relationship with their team. Take this seriously.

Anyone who refers you is putting their reputation in your hands. Show up on time. Be prepared. Be yourself.

Then, if that agent signs you, buy your friend a thank you gift or write them a nice card.

They just did you a huge favor.

Once you have an agent,
you have to motivate them.

It's like being in any relationship. It takes time, care, and attention. You must continue to lead, inspire, and nurture your team.

Don't expect them to do all the work while you wait for a phone call.
They make 10% of the money.
Expect them to do 10% of the work. You make 90% of the money.
You do 90% of the work.

Agents are most inspired by actors who are inspired. What you used to get your team is the same thing you will use to motivate them.
Work.
Keep working.
Keep inviting them.

When you make new contacts, tell them.
When you appreciate their help, tell them.

Develop a rapport with your team.

Remember significant dates, remember their children's names, remember their favorite book.

Write them hand written, "just because" letters, buy them small thank you gifts, and send them a kind text message out of the blue.

When you work, be happy to pay them.

And always, always, brag about them.

It's a small town.

I promise, someone is listening.

The Golden Rule:
Do unto others as you
would have them
do unto you.

The Diamond Rule:
Do unto others BETTER
than you would have
them do unto you.

When dealing with your team,
follow the diamond rule.

Reaching Out to Casting Directors

Casting Directors, Associates,
and Assistants work hard.

They hustle.

Casting Directors work job to job, contract to contract, just like you. Casting Directors are hired by producers to know, audition, and present the best actors in town. For most jobs, the Casting Director does not have final say on casting, the producer or director does.

There is an art to casting.

Casting Directors are fellow artists who navigate the same type of hustle that you navigate.

They are not your adversary.
They are not "gate keepers".

They are your greatest ally.
Your biggest champion.
And they want to know you.

When Reaching Out to Casting Directors, be specific about
who you are Reaching Out to.

Remember,
you don't belong on
every show or in every film.

Not every job is right for you, and not every Casting Director
is looking for you.

Do your research.

What 5 shows do you belong on?
Who is casting those shows?

Reach out to those
5 Casting Directors.

*a note to consider

Agents, Managers, and Casting Directors are many things, and play many roles. They pitch you. They negotiate for you. They advise you. They connect you. They champion you. They hustle for you.

But, be very clear, it's not their job
to teach you how to act.

Agents, Managers, and Casting Directors are not acting teachers.

They may recognize a good actor. They may appreciate a good actor. They may have excellent taste.

And while they may offer good notes, and you can learn from anyone, most are not qualified to be effective acting teachers. Just as you aren't qualified to be an agent, manager, or casting director.

Knowing a restaurant is good doesn't qualify you to train the chef.

Networking

In the Creative Economy,
it's not about who you
know, it's about who you
have a relationship with.

Relationships take
Patience
Hope
Generosity
Discipline

Relationships require that you
offer as much as you receive.

Stop thinking this question:

"I wonder what they can do for me?"

Start thinking this question:

"I wonder what I can do for them?"

Ground your Reaching Out in this question, and people will
start to notice something different about you.

Hearing No

When you Reach Out there is a word that will be said to you more than any other word. In fact, if you're working well, you will be told this word a lot. If you manage your time well, and you reach out for 13 hours a week, you will be told "No" at least 17 times in a week.

You will be told, "no",

but you do not have to hear, "no".

Your relationship to "no" will determine your happiness in this career. The good news is, there's a solution for every problem, and "no" is an invitation to discovering the solution.

"No" can mean any variation of "yes".

"No" might mean, "later", "next time", "try again", "get to know me more", "adjust the offer", "re-write the pitch".

There is always a path to "yes".

In a Creative Economy, "rejection"
is an event, not an identity.

Your offering may have been declined,
but you have not been.

Rejection, like a mistake, is like a comma. It may make you
pause, but it is not the end of the sentence.

You are the author of this career.

The industry gets to read what you author. They get to
comment on it. They may even get to play a role in your
story.

But you are the author.

It's ok to be disappointed.

But, never become discouraged.

Just
keep
writing
your
story.

*a note on Reaching Out

Remember that you are working in a Creative Economy.
Your Reaching Out must be supported by your Cause, your
Community, and your Practice.

You must continue to listen to the voices of Patience, Hope,
Generosity, and Discipline.

Define what success means to you, and stay in your personal,
professional, and communal integrity.

If your Reaching Out is always aligned with your Reaching
In, you will
never go off track.

Reaching To

This is the special sauce. This is the thing that will distinguish you from everyone else. This is the difference maker. This is the part that brings it all together and keeps you rooted in the stuff that actually matters.

This is the hardest part
with the greatest rewards.

This is Reaching To.

When you Reach To,
you extend your attention,
time, and effort to help others
without the expectation
of help in return.

Did you read that?

We do this WITHOUT
expectation of return.

Yes.

True service is offered for its own sake,
and offered to people without
catch, agenda, or
strings attached.

When you Reach To,
you ground your career in humility that

cultivates perspective
deepens relationships
nurtures your soul
and ignites your creativity.

Intentional Service to
others is the difference
between a good career and
a great career.

Service is the natural
condition of a grateful life.

And it is the context for
all lasting careers.

Whenever an actor sits with
me to discuss their acting career,
they often say they feel

stuck
down
unmotivated
frustrated
exhausted
depressed
confused
unfulfilled
lacking
bitter
ready to give up

I always ask the same question:

"Who are you serving?"

And I always get the same answer:

"No one."

Reaching To others is the fastest
way to reawaken the artist within.

The purest way to
develop relationships.

The surest
way to thrive

and

the best way to
be remembered.

It is the root of all
transformational
practice,

the core of
meaningful
community,

and

the catalyst for
a life of
cause.

The most artistic choice
you can ever make
is to work for the
benefit of others.

There are many ways to Reach To

Feed the hungry,
Help a friend run lines,
Clean the theatre (without being asked),
Buy tickets for your friend's play,
Shoot a self-tape audition for a friend,
Offer to give feedback on someone's headshots,
Help someone move,
Pay for dinner,
Intern at a casting office,
Give blood,
Offer to run the box office for a friend's play,
Volunteer with an organization,
Give to charity,
Free Listen with Urban Confessional...

No matter how you Reach To, the act of reaching to serve
someone will shift you from the inside out.

The cumulative effects of this shift will
always guide you deeper into
the Creative Economy.

When you Reach To others,
you move from a "Me" perspective to a "We" perspective.

It's like opening the aperture on a camera to let more light in.
The more light there is, the more you see.

The more you see, the more you perceive.

The more you perceive, the more affected you become.

The more affected you become, the more you come to life.

The more you come to life, the more you bring others to life.

The more you bring others to life, the more you see.

Reaching To and serving others opens the aperture of life and
starts a never-ending, life-
giving cycle of artistic growth.

Humility is the posture of all great

Leaders
Artists
Teachers
Actors

because humility is the
source of all risk.

When you have nothing to protect,
you have nothing to lose.

When you have nothing to lose,
you risk boldly.

When you serve others,
you build your capacity for risk
by increasing your
capacity for humility.

Humility is the root of presence,
the seed to openness,
and the glue for
togetherness.

It is the posture that allows you to learn,
to grow from mistakes,
and to treat
others with
respect.

It is an accurate assessment
of who you are
today.

It is not a false
undervaluation
of your worth.

Humility does not ask you to think less of yourself; but, to
think of yourself less.

It is the ultimate declaration of a worth not based in the
approval of others.

(read that again).

When you serve others,
you bring value to them.

When you bring value to them,
you become valuable to them.

When you become valuable to them,
they see your strengths, not your deficiencies.

This is how you shape your reputation in this industry.

This is a key ingredient to building a career in the Creative
Economy.

You create your significance by bringing significance to others.

Let's flip something on its head.

In many industries, powerful and significant people have assistants who get them coffee, buy their groceries, and pick their kids up from school.

Even at home, they have nannies, maids, and handymen. Someone cuts their grass, does their laundry, and cooks their food.

They are surrounded by people who jump at every command, and come to every call. How powerful they must be to have so many people serving them.

In the Corporate Economy, we see that power and significance is revealed by how many people serve you.

Let's flip this around.

In a Creative Economy, power and significance is revealed not in how many people serve you, but in how many people you serve.

You are powerful.

You are strong.

You have influence.

Do not use your strength to control;
use it to serve.

Do not use your power to oppress;
use it to empower.

Do not use your influence to manipulate;
use it to liberate.

Ultimately, your career will be
defined by how many
lives you enhanced,
not by how many
people enhanced
your life.

<u>Self-Care in Reaching To</u>

Many people misinterpret self-care. I have heard actors use "self-care" as the reason they do not Reach To.

They might say,

"I don't want to overdo myself. I'm already exhausted, I don't have time to help other people. I can barely help myself. I need to focus on myself. I need to do me."

This comes from a Corporate Economy mindset, and is a misunderstanding of the relationship between service and self-care.

Self-care is not a reason to avoid Reaching To. Instead, it is the means by which we continue to Reach To, and is a requirement for anyone living a life of service.

Your ability to Reach To is compromised if you never Reach In. And your ability to Reach In is compromised if you never Reach To.

Understand that serving others, Reaching To, is not about assuming their weight as yours.

In the Creative Economy, you do not assume the stress, fears, and responsibilities of another person. Instead, you offer to walk beside them, encourage them, empower them, and help them navigate.

You are not the doer, they are. You are not the hero in their story, they are.

You are not Reaching To in effort to fix them, but to love them.

You are accountable for your Reaching In, for your self-care. You are accountable for your Rest.

Make time for it, so you can freely make time for others.

ACTORS,

The Creative Economy is a life, not a study. Not a technique.
Not just a career approach.

It must be lived.

It must be renewed and never allowed to grow stale. If it
grows stale, it's no longer a life, it's a job.

It must be lived with others. No one achieves greatness
alone.

This is not going to get easier, but it will get better.

Your future is an option, not an obligation.

Choose your future.

In the end,

after the curtain closes,

after they call "cut!",

and after the lights dim,

there is only one thing remaining.

You.

Not your resume.

Not your reel.

Not your headshot.

You.

The greatest work of
art you will ever create is the
life you are living.

Keep your word,

honor your commitments,

love deeply, give freely,

express truthfully,

and listen openly.

Brag about others, serve the world,

keep your integrity,

call your parents sometimes,

and laugh a lot.

Be art before you do art, because at the end of the day,
the art you live will be reflected in the art you make,

and there is no greater work of art
than a life well lived.

About the Author

Benjamin Mathes has been an actor for over 25 years. On film, television, and stage he has worked with artists such as Clint Eastwood, Alan Arkin, Sam Raimi, Bradley Cooper, Andy Garcia, Chris Rock, and Brian Grazer. He received his MFA in Acting from the University of California, Irvine.

For 6 years he served as Head of Production for Seine Pictures, a film finance and production company in Hollywood. He Executive Produced the dark comedy, Murder of a Cat (starring Greg Kinnear, J.K. Simmons, and Nikki Reed), and the biopic, Pel (in partnership with Brian Grazer and Ron Howard's Imagine Entertainment). Both premiered at the Tribeca Film Festival.

As a teacher, he has been on faculty or taught workshops at Auburn University, Cal State Northridge, University of San Diego, University of Lima, Peru, Catholic University of Lima, University of California Irvine, Western Michigan University, Arizona State University, the Lincoln Center Director's Lab, and regularly runs actor's retreats in Ireland.

He is also a certified Associate Teacher of Fitzmaurice Voicework®, and has served as vocal and dialect coach for major motion pictures, network television, and theatres around the country.

His acting studio, CRASH ACTING, inspires a guerrilla approach to acting driven by the idea that service is the context for artistic greatness. His students have won or been nominated for Tony, Emmy, Grammy, and Ovation Awards, and have appeared on Broadway, as guest stars and series regulars on television, and in major motion pictures.

Benjamin is the author of two other books detailing and investigating the creative process. The first, Thought Lozenges for Artists, is a daringly optimistic, "open-where-you-want" look into the creative process, and the second, CRASH, Unstuck Yourself, is a guided journal designed to directly combat the blocks holding us from our creative potential.

Benjamin is the founder of Urban Confessional: A Free Listening Project. Currently in over 80 countries, their volunteers stand on street corners with signs that say "Free Listening" and provide compassionate, non-judgmental listening for anyone who needs to talk. Their work has been featured in over 40 national publications including the Huffington Post, The Atlantic, Fast Company, and The Big Think, as well as in over 30 international publications across 15 languages.

Notes

Notes

45742849R00167

Made in the USA
Columbia, SC
28 December 2018